Homemade

Recipes

Discover The Importance Of Healthy Dog Food & Make Your Own Natural Dog Food

(With 25 delicious & healthy homemade recipes!)

Bowe Packer

TABLE OF CONTENTS

PUBLISHERS NOTES

Disclaimer

This publication is intended to provide helpful and informative material. It is not intended to diagnose, treat, cure, or prevent any health problem or condition within your dog, nor is intended to replace the advice of a veterinarian.

No action should be taken solely on the contents of this book. Always consult your veterinarian on any matters regarding your dogs health and before adopting any suggestions in this book or drawing inferences from it.

The author and publisher specifically disclaim all responsibility for any liability, loss or risk, personal or otherwise, which is incurred as a consequence, directly or indirectly, from the use or application of any contents of this book.

Any and all product names referenced within this book are the trademarks of their respective owners. None of these owners have sponsored, authorized, endorsed, or approved this book.

Always read all information provided by the manufacturers' product labels before using their products. The author and publisher are not responsible for claims made by manufacturers.

Paperback Edition 2014

Manufactured in the United States of America

DEDICATION

I dedicate this book to all those people out there who remind us of the things we have forgotten about ourselves.

And this holds especially true of my beautiful and amazing wife, Alma. She is the one woman who has the most amazing talent to let me grow and love the things about myself that I have not fully accepted.

I cherish the love she has for me when I may not know how to love myself.

May we all have this kind of beautiful soul in our life.

Sent from LOVE,
Sunshine In My Soul

HOW TO USE THIS BOOK

This book is intended to help dog owners and dog lovers to keep their pets healthy by providing them with healthy, homemade meals. There are many different health problems that can affect dogs and many of those start with obesity and other dietary issues. This book is going to explain what you need to know about your dog's health and nutrition needs and then it's going to give you some excellent recipes to follow so your dog can get healthy, homemade, great tasting food.

We know a lot about proteins, fats and carbs for human consumption but do you know much about what your dog needs as far as these nutrients? Not to worry, we're going to tell you all about that and we're going to tell you all about the other nutrients and minerals that your dog may need as well. Plus, we have a great section on things that are dangerous for your dog so you don't have to worry about accidently causing more harm than good when you make your own foods.

PART I: INTRODUCTION

My family and I have always loved animals of all types. That meant we *had* a lot of animals as well and several of them were dogs. As a child and into adulthood I wanted to make sure that my dogs were well taken care of and that they had the best care possible. It's a goal that most everyone has. After all, who doesn't want to take good care of their pets? The problem is that a lot of people adopt pets without really knowing what it takes to look after them properly.

One of the most important things that you need to know about is the nutrition that your dog needs. There are actually a lot of things you want to make sure that your dog is getting and if you aren't looking into those things you could be hurting your dog more than you know. If you're feeding your dog just any national, commercial brand dog food off the shelf you could be hurting them as well because not all of those dog foods have the ingredients that your dog actually needs.

CHAPTER 1: WHERE COMMERCIAL DOG FOOD COMES FROM

Commercial dog food had to come from somewhere right? Just like everything else, at one point everyone just made their own and then one day someone decided to start making large quantities and sell it to the public. People who owned dogs before this would often give their pets their own food and table scraps as their meal which led to a lot of unhealthy pets.

Gradually people came to realize that dogs need to have special nutrition as well, just like people do. Otherwise your pets could end up with the same types of illnesses that humans get. It's actually possible for your dog to get hypertension, cancer and diabetes, did you know that? Well if you aren't careful it's very likely that it could happen to your dog.

Feeding dog's commercial pet food began around World War II. The Baby Boom had occurred and that meant there were a lot more people eating meat around the world. Because meat was being consumed more it needed to be processed even more. But when you process meat there are many byproducts that are created that can't (or won't) be eaten by people. These byproducts however, became the foundation for pet food.

R. Purina created an industrial process to mass produce feed for animals which originally began with hogs and chickens. By creating pellets that could be fed to these animals it was far easier to increase output of the animals. This also helped to get rid of the unusable byproducts of meat production (unusable by humans anyway). After some time the pet food companies began creating food for other animals such as dogs, cats and rabbits as well.

Dry foods use flour and animal meets as well as milk products to create a pellet that your pet can eat. Some also contain added vitamins and minerals to help make them healthier for your pets. If you're looking for more information on the contents of your dog's kibble you can know that it has at least 40% carbs because if it had less than the industrial process currently in use would not work.

The next type of dog food is the semi-moist food. It contains humectants to keep it moist and to keep it from spoiling at the same time. This product is actually a chemical compound which stops chemical processes from occurring that would typically cause spoiling of any kind of moist food product. It also contains ground soybeans and fresh meat. It may also contain some fat.

Finally, we have canned food. There are different types of this food which include rationed dog food (primarily made of meat scraps and internal organs cooked in a high pressure environment that creates a liquid state), all-meat (made of animal tissue and meat byproducts with added preservatives to maintain freshness) and chunky stews.

Did you know that some of the ingredients in your dog's food are put there just for you? Some of the color that appears in the food isn't natural at all and is actually added pigments and artificial colorants which make the food less healthy for your dog. Unfortunately it makes the food look better to you and that means more pet owners purchase it without realizing that they are hurting their pets by doing so.

CHAPTER 2: UNDERSTANDING YOUR DOG'S HEALTH

There are many nutrients that your dog, just like you, needs in order to stay healthy. That's why we're going to start out with a focus on those nutrients that will help your dog to continue growing and healing properly. These nutrients will also help them to live longer and to live a happier and healthier life as well. Your dog will definitely thank you for listening to their health care needs.

CHAPTER 3: ALL ABOUT PROTEIN

Any mammal in the world needs protein in order to grow and repair their body. It also helps to regulate other important biological processes. This means that it is essential to include in your dog's diet. It also means you must avoid too high carbs in exchange for that great protein. Make sure you're giving them plenty of protein especially when they are first weaned and when they are still young and growing.

On the other hand, too much protein can lead to health problems of its own. If you give your dog too much protein it could end up with kidney problems and even kidney failure. If there is too much protein in your dog's diet it may also lead to a change in their temper which means a friendly and happy dog could snap at people.

CHAPTER 4: WHAT ABOUT FATS?

Fats are considered to be the most problematic of all nutrients both for animals and for humans but this is not necessarily the case. Though they are considered to be the worst cause of obesity (which is true) they are also essential to the overall health of yourself and your pets. Too little fat can cause your dog to suffer from kidney problems as well as unhealthy skin and fur.

One of the best healthy fats available for your dog is omega fatty acids which are most prevalent in fish. So make sure you're getting your dog some fish in their diet or at least a supplement with omega fatty acids so that they will get the right amount of fats that they need. Without these fats your dog could end up looking and feeling pretty bad.

CHAPTER 5: CARBS FOR YOUR DOG

In order for your dog to continue being as active as ever you need to make sure they are getting the carbs they need. These carbs turn into energy and that means your dog will need at least 40-50% carbs within their diet.

For regular, commercial dog food there are cheap versions of carbs which are primarily starch. But your dog may have troubles with digesting some types of carbs. For example many dogs show signs of allergies to soybeans. These signs may appear as flatulence or indigestion. If your dog does have this type of allergy then you're going to want to look for a different type of dog food with regular or wheat flour rather than soybean. If you really want to do what's best for your dog then look into the recipes later on.

CHAPTER 6: INDIGESTION

Most dog foods that are commercially sold have an absolute minimum of 40% carb content. On the other hand some foods are considered to be 'light' or 'low-fat' but have up to 70% carb content. This means that they are dangerous for your dog and have far too much carb content for a typical dog's diet.

What we would consider 'ancient' diets for dogs would contain approximately 30% carb content which means that your dog doesn't need to get so much carb content from their diet. Remember that dogs are naturally carnivores and that means they have extensive digestive systems that can break down complex proteins. These are what's needed for your dog to continue to have enough energy and biological maintenance.

When dogs have food allergies it can cause them indigestion. On the other hand if they don't have the right number of digestive enzymes or have the wrong types of sugar or carbs in their system. These things can cause enzyme deficiencies and this causes foods to be improperly digested. When the food remains in the digestive tract it begins to ferment and create bacteria.

This causes indigestion for the dog which is also affected by several other factors:

- The dogs age
- Infection of the digestive tract
- Intestinal inflammation

Chapter 7: Micronutrients

Vitamins and minerals are incredibly important to dogs just like they are to humans. You need to ensure that they are getting the trace nutrients that they need to grow and to ensure tissue repair and metabolic regulation. If they don't get these nutrients from their traditional diet then you need to ensure that they are getting it in another way.

If your dog has a vitamin deficiency then make sure you visit with a veterinarian. They are the only ones that are going to be able to diagnose any type of problem your dog may have. Don't try to diagnose your pets yourself as this can be very problematic for your dog. A professional can diagnose health problems and will be able to determine if any trouble your dog is having is related to a vitamin deficiency or if it is a bigger problem that needs to be taken care of.

If your vet recommends supplements then take these things into account:

1. Dogs with bone injuries need calcium and phosphorus. These should be balanced out properly so your dog doesn't get too much of either mineral.

2. Pregnant dogs do need vitamin C but make sure you aren't giving them too much. This can simply be useless for dogs if it's too much.

3. If your dog has trouble with dry or scaly skin because of humidity or temperature changes you may want to provide them with vitamin E supplements. This will help to provide cell regeneration as well as a cleaner and healthier coat.

4. If your dog has stress problems or flea infestation then you want B-complex supplements. This will ensure they are healthier and feeling better as well.

   Vitamins A, D, E, and K are fat-soluble and will help with blood clotting, bleeding, improving eyesight and aiding in bone repair. If your dog has a deficiency in these vitamins it can cause:

1. Weak muscles

2. Inability to reproduce

3. Weak immune system

4. Vision problems

5. Rickets

Vitamins in the B complex family are important to the health of any dog but that doesn't mean that you should keep giving your dog more and more vitamins. Too much of a good thing is actually a bad thing. That's because overabundance of vitamins can lead to:

- Clarification of vital organs

- Severe bone problems

CHAPTER 8: GIVING YOUR DOG MINERALS

All minerals produce benefits to your dog in the following ways:

Minerals	Benefits
Calcium	Normal growth and repair of bones
Phosphorous	Normal growth and repair of bones
Potassium	Cellular maintenance, kidney health, muscle maintenance
Sodium	Prevents dehydration
Magnesium	Needed for the normal

	functioning of vital organs like the heart
Iron	Needed for production and maintenance of red blood cells
Zinc	Needed for healthy fur and normal skin
Copper	Copper is used by the dog's body to maintain a healthy coat. Copper is also needed to utilize the mineral *iron*.

CHAPTER 9: PHOSPHORUS & CALCIUM

These two minerals need to be balanced. But how do you know how much you should be giving and what true balance really is? Well it's actually right here in this chart.

Time in the Dog's Life	Percentage of Calcium	Percentage of Phosphorous
During pregnancy	1% to 1.8%	.8% to 1.6%
Growing years	1% to 1.8%	.8% to 1.6%
"Teenage" years	.8% to 1.5%	.6% to 1.2%
Before giving birth to puppies	.8% to 1.5%	.6% to 1.2%
Regular adult	.5% to .9%	.4% to .8%

Chapter 10: What About Zinc?

Zinc will keep your dog's coat going strong and it will keep their skin healthy as well. Not only this it will be important to growing pups, pregnant dogs and working dogs. Below we will inform you of the minimum amount and the maximum amount that your dog needs. Remember that too much zinc can be toxic and that's why it's important to stick at or below the maximum levels of zinc.

Stage in the Dog's Life	Minimum Amount of Zinc	Maximum Amount of Zinc
Young puppy & growing dogs	120 mg/kg	1,000 mg/kg
Adult dogs (non-reproducing)	120 mg/kg	1,000 mg/kg

Working dogs & performance dogs	150 mg/kg	300 mg/kg

Remember that different foods have different contents of zinc in them. That means you need to make sure that you are getting only as much zinc as your dog needs and no more. This means understanding how much zinc is in each of those different foods:

Food Item	Zinc Content
Barley	44.4 mg/kg
Corn	13 mg/kg
Oats	39.2 mg/kg

Bowe Packer

Rice	24.4 mg/kg
Wheat	20 mg/kg
Soybean meal	57.9 mg/kg
Fish meal	157 mg/kg
Meat & bone meal	101 mg/kg

CHAPTER 11: CANINE DIET

1. Palatability is important for your dog. If they don't think the food looks attractive then, just like you, they won't eat it. This means you need to make the food look good no matter what it is.

2. Watch your pet to see if they are digesting their food well. This is especially important if your dog is trying out some new food. If they are doing well after their meals then you want to make sure they are eating properly as well. If they have indigestion after they eat it could be because they are allergic to the food. Make sure you change out the food immediately.

3. If your dog has a change in their activity level then you want to make sure you are looking into what's causing it. Your dog may be a very calm dog anyway and this is fine (as long as you've had your vet check them out and discovered nothing wrong). On the other hand if your dog is normally active and suddenly becomes lethargic you'll want to check it out immediately.

CHAPTER 12: CALORIE TRACKING

Your dog probably likes snacks but it's important that you keep track of how many snacks they are given. This allows you to keep your dog's calorie intake down to an acceptable level. Keep in mind also that it's important to keep your dog from getting table scraps as this can lead to high calorie levels and obesity.

Treat	Calories
Small, bite-sized dog biscuits	5 calories
Medium-sized dog biscuits	20 calories
Premium dog biscuits ("gourmet biscuits") for small dogs	70 calories
"Light" dog biscuits	15 calories

Baby carrot	3 calories
8 ounces of green beans	25 calories
.5 ounces of popcorn	54 calories
1 regular slice of cheese pizza	259 calories
1 small serving of cheese-coated French fries	399 calories
1 regular chocolate chip cookie	180 calories
1 small serving of soft ice cream	113 calories

Bowe Packer

1 large hamburger with cheese	525 calories

CHAPTER 13: NEWBORN PUPS

If your dog has pups you want to make sure that it's getting the proper food and nutrition that will keep it healthy and growing properly. This will change from day one until the dog is old enough to eat just like the rest of your dogs. You'll want to watch out for the new mother dog as well since she will need special care.

Day 1-The pup is gone and the newborn with suckle from the mother. These pups will feed every three hours and should be firm and full of milk at all times. They will gain weight as time goes on though they may lose a little within the first days after they are born. After this initial weight loss however they should begin to gain weight and continue gaining.

Day 2-3-The mother dog will begin to feed at this point. Make sure that you are not feeding them normal foods as this is not going to be healthy for her or for her pups. Instead, you want to provide her with a mash or high fat, protein and carb diet.

Bowe Packer

Week 3-At this point the puppy will start to pay attention to its food. You want to make sure that you are giving them only as much water as they need and that they are beginning to show an interest in food. You can also start giving them dry puppy food mashed with dog milk replacement. You should blend the two together into a smooth consistency.

Week 6-7-About this time you want to make sure your puppy is being weaned off its mother's milk. You can start giving them dry puppy food and clear water. You're also going to want to give the mother regular food once again since this will help to slow her production of milk which assists with the weaning process.

CHAPTER 14: MINIMUM NUTRIENTS

There are some minimum requirements that are actually published by the Association of American Feed Control Officials. This doesn't necessarily mean that all dog food brands contain these levels however so make sure you are checking any commercial food. You want to compare to this chart to determine what you dog needs and what they are getting.

Note: mg/kg is the ration for minimum amount per kilogram of body weight for your dog. Keep this in mind as you feed your dog.

Nutrient	Percentage / Amount Needed by Young Dogs and Pregnant Dogs	Percentage/Amount Needed by Adult Dogs (Non-Reproducing)
Choline	1,200 mg/kg	1,200 mg/kg

Bowe Packer

Cyanobalamin	0.022 mg/kg	0.022 mg/kg
Folic acid	0.18 mg/kg	0.18 mg/kg
Pyroxidine	1 mg/kg	1 mg/kg
Niacin	11.4 mg/kg	11.4 mg/kg
Pantothenic acid	10 mg/kg	10 mg/kg
Riboflavin	2.2 mg/kg	2.2 mg/kg
Thiamin	1 mg/kg	1 mg/kg
Vitamin E	50 mg/kg	50 mg/kg
Vitamin D	500 mg/kg	500 mg/kg
Vitamin A	5,000 IU/kg	5,000 IU/kg
Selenium	0.11 mg/kg	0.11 mg/kg
Iodine	1.5 mg/kg	1.5 mg/kg
Zinc	120 mg/kg	120 mg/kg
Manganese	5 mg/kg	5 mg/kg
Copper	7.3 mg/kg	7.3 mg/kg

Iron	80 mg/kg	80 mg/kg
Magnesium	0.04%	0.04%
Chloride	0.45%	0.09%
Sodium	0.3%	0.06%
Potassium	0.6%	0.6%
Calcium	1%	0.6%
Phosphorous	0.8%	0.5%
Linoleic acid	1%	1%
Fat content	8%	5%
Valine	.48%	.39%
Tryptophan	.2%	.16%
Threonine	.58%	.48%
Phenylalanine -tyrosine	0.89%	0.73%
Methionine- cystine	0.53%	0.43%

Bowe Packer

Lysine	0.77%	0.63%
Leucine	0.72%	0.59%
Isoleucine	0.45%	0.37%
Histidine	0.22%	0.18%
Arginine	0.62%	0.51%
Protein	22%	18%

CHAPTER 15: TOXIC FOODS FOR DOGS

Humans can eat many different types of foods that dogs really can't. Because of this you need to understand the biological chemistry of your dog and you need to make sure that you are avoiding the foods listed on the chart below so that you keep your dog healthy.

Food Item	Reason Why It Should Not Be Given to Dogs
Beer, whiskey, rum, or any alcoholic beverage	Alcohol can cause severe intoxication in dogs, which can lead to death. It's been documented that some dogs given alcoholic beverages have gone into comas.
Avocado	All the parts of the avocado plant, including the fruit,

	contain the chemical compound *persin,* which has been known to cause vomiting and even loose bowel movements in dogs.
Hard bones from animals like chickens	Contrary to some popular beliefs, dogs *cannot* break down hard bones. Like humans, dogs can suffer from a punctured stomach from eating bones.
Commercial cat food	Generally, commercial cat food contains higher protein content than regular dog food. Some experts believe that higher concentrations of protein can cause

	kidney failure in dogs.
Chocolate and caffeinated beverages	Although chocolate tastes good, it contains the compound theobromine. Dogs are unable to metabolize theobromine. Over time, this chemical compound can accumulate in a dog's system until a toxic level is reached. Caffeine, as well as the chemical theophylline, is present in coffee, coffee-based beverages, and teas. Both these

	compounds can affect the dog's heart and may also cause vomiting in some cases.
Citrus oil	Citrus oil has been known to cause vomiting in dogs.
Pure fat cut from beef or pork	Too much fat can cause pancreatitis, a severe condition in both humans and dogs.
Large amounts of fish (in whatever form)	If the dog is not given sources of protein other than fish, the dog can suffer from vitamin deficiency (thiamine deficiency, to be exact).
Grapes and other grape-derived	An unknown toxin in the flesh of grapes has

snacks and food items	been known to cause kidney problems. The same goes for currants, so don't give your dog's fresh or cooked currants.
Hops (grain)	An unknown toxin in this grain causes severe allergic reactions in dogs. Documented reactions include elevated heart rate, difficulty breathing, and even death. Some dogs have been known to suffer from seizures.
Vitamin supplements for humans (with iron)	Human vitamin supplements that contain the mineral iron can cause havoc

	in the digestive tract of dogs. Organs like the liver -- and even the dog's kidneys -- can also take damage.
Macadamia nuts (fresh or otherwise)	These nuts have been known to damage the central nervous system of dogs. They may also adversely affect the digestive system.
Marijuana	Can cause vomiting and cardiovascular problems.
Spoiled food and table scraps	High levels of bacteria and molds in spoiled food can cause food poisoning and kill a dog.
Wild mushrooms	May contain potent toxins that can

	paralyze and kill a dog immediately after consumption.
Onions	Affect the red blood cells of dogs and also deplete the iron supply of the animal.
Persimmons	When ingested, the seeds of the persimmon can cause inflammation in the digestive tract and may also cause severe obstructions.
Raw eggs	Raw eggs contain the compound called avidin, which has been known to prevent the complete absorption and utility of the nutrient biotin. If given in large

	amounts, raw eggs can cause biotin deficiency, which can have a negative impact on the dog's skin and coat.
Rhubarb leaves	Oxalates found in rhubarb leaves can attack multiple organ systems, including the dog's central nervous system.
Salt	Large amount of salt can destroy a dog's delicate chemical balance.
Food items and treats with lots of table sugar	Too much sugar in a dog's diet can cause dental problems and can also lead to obesity.
Table scraps	Table scraps often

	contain fat and salt, and are generally empty calories with little or no nutritive value.
Yeast dough	Increases gas production in the dog's bowels, which can cause internal rupturing and death.
Xylitol	If given in excessive amounts, can cause hypoglycemia. Hypoglycemia in dogs can cause vomiting. If xylitol reaches a toxic level in the dog's system, the dog's liver may shut down completely.

Chapter 16: Growth Rates

Do you know how big your dog will get? Well there are actually many different types of dogs and each will grow to a different size. Understanding how large your dog should be will help you to keep them from being obese or underweight.

Toy Dogs-Below ten pounds until approximately four months than ten pounds through adulthood.

Cocker Spaniel- Ten pounds around four months then 18-20 pounds through adulthood.

Bulldog-Below 20 pounds at four months, 20 pounds at eight months, 30 pounds at 12 months, below 40 pounds until 16 months and then approximately 40 pounds from 20 months on up.

Setters-30 pounds at four months, 45 pounds around eight months, 45+ pounds at 12 months and 48+ pounds throughout adulthood.

German Shepherd-45 pounds at four months, 60+ pounds at eight months and 70 pounds from 12 months through adulthood.

Great Dane-70 pounds at four months, 90+ pounds around eight months, 110+ pounds around 12 months and 130 pounds from 16 months until adulthood.

CHAPTER 17: FEEDING OLDER DOGS

When your dog starts getting older you want to make sure that you are taking good care of them. This means that you are getting them the healthy and nutritious food that they need. As dogs get older it can be more difficult to get them to eat properly and that means your dog could get obese or malnourished. So what should you do?

1. Senior dogs need a different type of diet. They may also need to eat different amounts and at a different level of frequency than younger dogs. This means ensuring that you keep track of what your dog is eating and how often so that you can adjust their diet to their new needs.

2. Older dogs will need softer foods and will also need less sugary treats. This is because their teeth and gums are weaker and have a better chance of developing cavities. Try to avoid as many treats as possible for your dog when they are older because of these things.

3. If your dog is getting less exercise (a common plight with older dogs) you need to make sure that they are eating less food than they were when they were more active.

4. Make sure that you are getting enough fiber into your dog's food so that they are getting a better digestive health level. You want to get them around 3-5% fiber in their diet with less fat content than you would give to a younger dog.

5. If your dog is not interested in their food this could be because of the size or portions they are getting. It could also be due to the fact that the food is too difficult for them to eat and they need softer food with more moisture.

CHAPTER 18: SWITCHING YOUR DOG'S DIET

Changes need to be done slowly in your dog's diet. If you make a very sudden change in your dog's diet you could cause them health problems such as indigestion. This occurs because your dog ends up with a change intestinal flora that has to happen extremely quickly. Gradual changes on the other hand should take place over five days or more and they should be done to the needs of your dog.

For older dogs the transition period should definitely be longer. You will want to wait at least ten days to make a full transition because your dog will have more trouble digesting their food and will likely also have more trouble with indigestion and allergies. If you follow the chart below your dog should be fine with the transition.

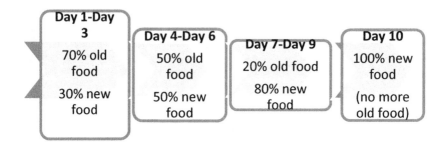

Day 1-Day 3	Day 4-Day 6	Day 7-Day 9	Day 10
70% old food	50% old food	20% old food	100% new food
30% new food	50% new food	80% new food	(no more old food)

CHAPTER 19: ARE YOU GIVING YOUR DOG ENOUGH WATER?

Make sure that your dog is getting plenty of water which is typically going to be 1 bowl of water for every pound of food that they eat. This will help them get the water that they need. You'll also want to change this up if the dog is pregnant because they will need to get more water in their system.

If your dog is sick then make sure they are getting plenty of clean and clear water. If they are vomiting make sure you aren't giving them too much water because this can actually increase the trouble that they are having. Make sure you give your vet a call when you do this as well to ensure that they are getting the nutrition they need.

PART 2: SNACKS MADE AT HOME

If you have a dog at home you know how expensive it can be to buy food for them all the time. But it's not just the expense that you should consider. There's the health of your dog as well. Making your own dog food can be cheaper (though not necessarily) but it's definitely healthier for your dog. Of course before you even consider it you should be thinking about a few important pros and cons. You should also consider these reasons why other people have decided to make their own dog food.

1. Their dog needs a special diet to counter health conditions.
2. The dog is in training and needs added protein or calories.
3. The dog is allergic to a product found in most dog food.
4. The dog is unable to digest regular dog food.
5. The owner has decided it's healthier for the dog to eat homemade food.

For myself I like to give my dog homemade meals because it allows them to get the right balance of proteins, fats and carbs. I can also control what goes into the food and how much they eat. In this section we outline some great recipes that you can try for your dog. You may need to experiment a little to find one that you think is right for your dog and that they enjoy but it will be worth it.

Make sure, while you're looking out for your dog's health, you're also looking out for a few common mistakes that many dog owners and lovers often make.

1. **Giving your dog table scraps.** These are actually very bad for your dog because they are full of empty calories and a lot of unhealthy ingredients. Your dog needs vitamins and minerals, not leftover bacon off your table.

2. **Jumping into a new diet.** Make sure that you are talking with your vet before you switch your dog from commercial dog food to homemade dog food. This way you can be sure that they are getting the vitamins and minerals they need to stay healthy.

3. **Sticking with the same thing.** Make sure you keep an eye on what's going on with the current state of research into dog's needs. You want to make sure that you know everything there is about how to keep your dog healthy and happy.

4. **Cook Properly.** If you don't cook your dog's food properly it could end up unsafe and if you aren't storing it properly it will go bad much faster. Make sure you are taking care of your dog the best way possible by taking care of their food.

5. **Transition slowly.** If your dog has been on a specific type of food for a long time you need to make sure you aren't jumping into anything new too quickly as this could cause your dog to get sick. You need to slowly transition them into a new type of food as we mentioned earlier.

CHAPTER 20: TREATS GALORE

If you want to give your dogs a healthy treat, pick from one of these great recipes!

Creamy Banana Treat

Ingredients:

- *Half cup of regular peanut butter*
- *3 bananas*
- *2 eggs*
- *2 tablespoons of honey*
- *1 cup of water (you can add milk if the dog tolerates dairy products)*
- *2 cups of flour (use wheat flour if available)*
- *1 teaspoon of baking powder*

Steps:

1. First, preheat your oven to 350 degrees Fahrenheit.

2. Combine all of the ingredients and mix well, until a smooth consistency is achieved.

3. On a medium-sized baking tray, place a cookie sheet and spread it evenly across the whole surface of the baking tray. Don't forget to spray the cookie sheet.

4. With a spoon or scoop, transfer the mixture to the cookie sheet, one spoonful/scoopful at a time.

5. Bake for a quarter of an hour and serve. The cookies can be placed in a sealed jar. They can also be frozen and served over the course of weeks.

Honey & Carob Delight

Ingredients:

- *Half cup of carob chips*
- *1 teaspoon of vanilla flavoring*
- *2 eggs*
- *Quarter cup of honey*
- *Quarter cup of canola oil*
- *Quarter cup of water (or fresh milk)*
- *Half cup of ground oats*
- *Two cups of flour (wheat flour, if available)*

Steps:

1. First, preheat the oven to 350 degrees Fahrenheit.

2. Combine all the ingredients in a non-reactive mixing bowl.

3. Spread a cookie sheet or baking sheet across your baking tray. Coat the sheet with non-stick spray.

4. Transfer the mixture to the cookie sheet. Place your cookies two to three inches apart.

5. Bake for a quarter of an hour and serve.

Brown Rice Cookies

Ingredients:

- *Half cup of boiled chicken (shred the chicken first)*
- *Whole cup of brown rice (cook the brown rice before making the cookies)*
- *2 tablespoons of regular honey*
- *2 tablespoons of canola oil*
- *1 egg*
- *Half cup of baby food (anything with chicken in the label)*
- *Half cup of chicken stock*
- *¼ teaspoon of salt*
- *1 teaspoon of baking powder*
- *Quarter cup of skim milk*
- *Two cups of flour (wheat flour if available)*

Steps:

- Preheat your oven to 350 degrees Fahrenheit.

- Combine most of the ingredients except the rise. Stir until well blended.

- Add the mixture to the rise and slowly mix, taking care to integrate a little air to the mixture.

- Apply large drops of the mix to a pre-sprayed baking tray with a cookie sheet.

- Bake for a quarter of an hour and serve.

Doggy Delight Cookies

Ingredients:

- *¼ teaspoon of salt*
- *1 teaspoon of baking powder*
- *Half cup of cornmeal*
- *Two cups of flour (if available, use wheat flour)*
- *One clove of fresh garlic*
- *2 tablespoons of canola oil*
- *1 egg*
- *Half cup of chicken broth (beef broth can also be used)*
- *Half cup of carrots (steamed or boiled carrots will do)*
- *Half cup of chicken (or any cooked poultry; shred the meat before using)*
- *Whole cup of mashed potatoes*

Bowe Packer

Steps:

1. Preheat oven to 350 degrees Fahrenheit.

2. Combine all the ingredients and mix thoroughly in a large mixing bowl.

3. Spread a cookie sheet over a baking tray and spray with non-stick. Form small dollops of the mixture to make the cookies.

4. Bake the cookies for at least twenty minutes. Serve.

Dog Food With a Touch of Home

Ingredients:

- *1 tablespoon of regular honey*
- *1 tablespoon of canola oil*
- *1 egg*
- *Half cup of chicken broth (beef broth can also be used)*
- *300-400 grams of dog food (wet or moist variety)*
- *¼ teaspoon of salt*
- *½ teaspoon of garlic powder*
- *Half cup of milk (use skim milk or low fat milk if available)*
- *Two cups of flour (use wheat flour if available)*

Steps:

1. Preheat oven to 350 degrees Fahrenheit.

2. Combine all the ingredients except the milk and flour in a large mixing bowl. Prepare the flour mixture next by mixing skim milk and the wheat flour (or regular flour). Add the first mix to the second mix. Combine both groups of ingredients well until a smooth and even consistency is achieved.

3. Place small dollops of the mix on a baking tray. Don't forget to spray the cookie sheet with non-stick spray. If the dough seems too thin or light, add more flour. You can flatten the dough with a glass or a rolling pin.

4. Bake the cookies for at least twenty minutes. To test for doneness, try to crack a cookie open. If the cookie is already springy, it's ready to serve.

Cheddar Dog Cookies

Ingredients:

-   *2 tablespoons of canola oil*
-   *Whole cup of chicken stock*
-   *Whole cup of cheddar cheese, grated*
-   *¼ teaspoon of salt*
-   *¼ teaspoon of garlic powder*
-   *2 teaspoons of basil*
-   *1 tablespoon of baking powder*
-   *Two cups of flour*

Steps:

1. Preheat your oven to 400 degrees Fahrenheit.

2. Combine all the ingredients except the canola oil and the chicken stock.

3. Spread a sprayed cookie sheet over the baking tray before applying the mix. Create half-inch cookies on the cookie sheet.

4. Bake the cookies for a quarter of an hour. The cookies will turn golden yellow when done.

Bowe Packer

Walnut & Cinnamon Express

Ingredients:

- *Half cup of walnuts, chopped*
- *Whole apple (shred or grate the apple)*
- *1 whole egg*
- *2 tablespoons of canola oil*
- *2 tablespoons of honey*
- *1 cup of water*
- *¼ teaspoon of salt*
- *¼ teaspoon of cinnamon*
- *1 teaspoon of baking soda*
- *2 cups of flour*

Steps:

1. Combine everything except the flour and the water. Combine the flour and water in a separate bowl. Add the first mix to the second bowl (the flour mix), and stir until a smooth consistency is achieved. Add the chopped walnuts and grated apple last.

2. Make half-inch dough drops on a baking tray lined with a cookie sheet. Pre-spray the cookie sheet before using.

3. Bake the cookies for at least twenty minutes. This recipe is suggested for dogs that need vitamin E supplementation, since *tocopherol*, or vitamin E, is a naturally occurring trace nutrient in walnuts. You can also add cheese to the mix if you wish.

Cookies for Healthy Eyes

Is your dog having trouble with his coat *and* eyesight? Try my *Cookies for Healthy Eyes* – the recipe is full of vitamin A -- delivered the way your dog wants it, through yummy cookies!

Ingredients:

- *1 carrot, grated*
- *1 whole egg*
- *2 tablespoons of molasses*
- *2 tablespoons of canola oil*
- *Half cup of water*
- *Whole can of pumpkin*
- *½ teaspoon of cinnamon*
- *1 teaspoon of baking soda*

Bowe Packer

- *2 cups of flour*

Steps:

1. Preheat your oven to 350 degrees Fahrenheit.

2. Combine all the ingredients except the flour and water. Create the primary flour mix in another bowl then add the first mix to the flour mix.

3. Prepare the baking tray by spraying a cookie sheet with non-stick spray. Add small dollops of the final mix to create the cookies.

4. Bake the cookies for twenty minutes and serve.

Sweet Potato Surprise

Ingredients:

- *Whole cup of cottage cheese*
- *Whole cup of mashed sweet potatoes (if sweet potatoes are not available, you can use a ready-made can of pumpkin puree or pumpkin chunks instead)*
- *1 egg*

- *2 tablespoons of canola oil*
- *2 tablespoons of regular honey*
- *Half cup of milk*
- *½ teaspoon of cinnamon (this flavoring is optional)*
- *1 teaspoon of baking powder*
- *2 cups of oats (instant oats)*
- *2 cups of flour*

Steps:

1. Preheat your oven to 350 degrees Fahrenheit.

2. Combine all the ingredients except the flour and milk. Combine the flour and milk in a large mixing bowl and *add* the first mix to the flour mix.

3. Stir the final mixture until smooth.

4. Place small dollops of the final mixture onto a non-stick baking tray.

5. Bake the cookies for at least twenty minutes before serving or storing.

Snacks and Quick Meals

Bowe Packer

Nutmeg Pudding

Ingredients:

- ¼ teaspoon of nutmeg (fresh, if possible)
- ¼ teaspoon of salt
- 2 eggs
- 2 tablespoons of regular honey
- 2 tablespoons of table sugar or molasses
- Half cup of cornmeal
- Two cups of milk

Steps:

1. Preheat your oven to 350 degrees.

2. Pour two cups of milk into a pot or saucepan. Switch the stove to medium heat. Let the milk simmer and eventually come to a boil.

3. When the milk starts boiling, reduce the stove's heat and slowly add the cornmeal. Stir regularly so that the cornmeal integrates well with the milk.

4. Add the sweetening agents (molasses/table sugar & honey) and the nutmeg. Lastly, add the two eggs (beat these first before using) and the ¼ teaspoon of salt.

5. Use a baking dish for this recipe. Bake for at least one hour before serving. The Nutmeg Pudding should be served warm (not chilled), or at least at room temperature.

Maple Appetizer

This recipe is suggested for dogs who are just recovering from illness or injury. Dogs who are just recovering usually have low or *no* appetites at all.

This light and very nutritious recipe will ensure that your dog gets a boosted dose of B-complex vitamins to help speed up recovery. This Maple Appetizer is also a good alternative snack for dogs that are allergic to food items with wheat, since millet is *not* related to wheat and does not contain compounds like gluten.

Ingredients:

- *½ teaspoon of cloves (ground)*
- *Whole teaspoon of cinnamon*

Bowe Packer

- *Half cup of maple syrup*
- *¼ teaspoon of salt*
- *Three cups of water*
- *Whole cup of millet*

Steps:

1. Preheat your oven to 350 degrees Fahrenheit.

2. Brush fresh butter over a medium-sized baking dish.

3. Cook the ingredients in a saucepan before pouring them into the baking dish. When the ingredients come to a boil, the mix is ready for the oven.

4. Bake the pudding mix for at least forty-five minutes before serving warm.

Tofu & Honey Heaven

Tofu is produced from soybean, one of the top sources of usable protein in the vegetable kingdom. You can give *Tofu & Honey Heaven* as a special treat to your dog. If your dog already has enough calories in his diet for the day, reduce the honey content of the treat by half.

Ingredients:

- *Half cup of regular honey*
- *Two cups of canola oil*
- *3 tablespoons of sesame seeds (for sprinkling)*
- *2 tablespoons of cornstarch*
- *Sixteen ounces of fresh tofu*

Steps:

1. Slice the tofu into regular, thin pieces. Fry both sides of each slice of tofu until you achieve a golden brown color. The tofu slices should also be a little crunchy, but not too dry.

2. Drain the oil from the tofu by applying paper towels.

3. Place all the cooked tofu in your dog's dish or bowl. Pour the honey *over* the cooked tofu slices.

4. Sprinkle three tablespoons of cornstarch over the finished snack.

Sweet Pumpkin Snack

Bowe Packer

Ingredients:

- *Half cup of sliced apples*
- *Quarter cup of honey*
- *Half cup of water*
- *Whole pumpkin (a medium-sized pumpkin will do)*

Steps:

1. Preheat your oven to 350 degrees Fahrenheit.

2. Slice the whole pumpkin in two. Remove the seeds and any stringy material you may find inside. Wash the pumpkin thoroughly to remove any chemicals from the skin. Do not remove the skin of the pumpkin as this is a good source of dietary fiber.

3. Slice the pumpkin into cubes – each cube should be about 1 ½ to 2 inches long.

4. Combine honey and water in a medium saucepan. Cook until smooth, honeyed syrup is formed.

5. When the syrup is done, add the sliced apples and cook for ten minutes or less. Do not overcook, as the sugar in the honey can burn easily in high temperatures.

6. Place all the pumpkin slices in a baking bowl or baking dish and bake for at least one hour.

7. When the pumpkin is done, pour the apple and honey mix on top and serve warm.

Spicy Pie

Ingredients:

- *1 pie crust (at least nine inches across)*
- *Quarter teaspoon of cloves (ground)*
- *Quarter teaspoon of ginger (ground)*
- *Half teaspoon of allspice (ground)*
- *Quarter teaspoon of salt*
- *2 whole eggs (separate the yolk from the egg white)*
- *Three sweet potatoes (cook these first before using)*

Steps:

1. Preheat your oven to 350 degrees Fahrenheit.

2. Remove the skin of the cooked sweet potatoes.

3. In a mixing bowl, mash the sweet potatoes until all chunks have disappeared.

4. Add two egg yolks to the sweet potatoes, along with the threes spices.

5. Place egg whites in a separate bowl and beat with a fork or hand-held beater until stiff peaks are formed.

6. Add one tablespoon of the beaten egg whites to the cooked sweet potato mix.

7. Pour the mix unto the pie crust and flatten evenly with a spoon.

8. Bake for at least forty minutes, slice and serve.

Beef & Cabbage Salad

Ingredients:

- *Quarter cup of parsley*
- *5 cooked potatoes (use small or young potatoes)*
- *Whole cup of beef (cooked well)*
- *Half a cabbage (shred the cabbage first)*
- *¼ teaspoon of salt*
- *Quarter cup of balsamic vinegar*
- *Egg yolk*
- *1 teaspoon of mustard or Dijon mustard*
- *1 teaspoon of garlic (minced finely)*
- *1 cup of olive oil*

Steps:

1. Create the dressing for this salad by combining egg yolk and all the other ingredients, except the cabbage and potatoes.

2. Arrange the pieces of cabbage and sliced potatoes on a plate. Add the beef next.

3. Pour the dressing over the finished salad and serve.

Doggy Tuna Salad

This recipe is recommended for overweight dogs that have been given a high-fat diet for a long time. Overweight dogs usually have a shorter lifespan than average-weight or optimum-weight dogs, which is why it's a good idea to start trimming excess weight *now*, while your dog is still strong.

Ingredients:

- *7 ounces of canned tuna*
- *1 teaspoon of sugar*
- *1 tablespoon of mustard or Dijon mustard*
- *Quarter cup of red wine vinegar*
- *Half cup of olive oil*
- *Quarter cup of white onion optional; if your dog does not like onions, do not add chopped onions to the Doggy Tuna Salad)*
- *1 medium-sized carrot (slice the carrot first)*
- *Whole head of cabbage*

Bowe Packer

Steps:

1. Remove the water from the tuna and pour the flakes in a separate container.

2. Combine the onions, sugar, and other ingredients with the tuna flakes.

3. Arrange the cabbage leaves in a bowl.

4. Top the cabbage leaves with the first mixture and serve to your dog.

Baked Veggie Roll

Ingredients:

- *Half cup of cheddar cheese, grated*
- *Whole cup of stock (chicken or beef)*
- *Half cup of yogurt (low fat variety)*
- *Pinch of ground pepper (black or white)*
- *¼ teaspoon of salt*
- *½ teaspoon of oregano*
- *1 teaspoon of parsley (use fresh parsley if available)*
- *Whole cup of rice (cook the rice before using)*
- *Whole cup of chicken (cooked; shredded)*
- *Separated cabbage leaves (7 to 10 leaves will do)*

Steps:

1. Preheat your oven to 350 degrees Fahrenheit. Use the largest baking dish you have.

2. Remove the hard portion of the separated cabbage leaves. Fill a pot with water and bring the water to a boil. When the water is already boiling, add the cabbage leaves.

3. Allow the cabbage leaves to soften enough so you can easily roll the leaves without breaking apart the leaf's structure.

4. Line a bowl or large plate with paper towels and transfer each of the simmered leaves unto the paper towel lining. Allow the paper towels to absorb the moisture.

5. Combine all the other ingredients in a mixing bowl. Mix well.

6. To bind the ingredients together, use the low fat yogurt. Add just enough of this ingredient to produce a thick mix. (Too much yogurt will cause the mix to fall apart when molded with the cabbage leaves.)

7. For each cabbage leaf, add two to three tablespoonsful of the primary roll mix.

8. Roll each filled cabbage leaf, taking care to 'lock' the cabbage leaf by tucking in the corners.

9. Place the rolled cabbage leaves in a baking dish, side by side.

10. Pour the stock of your choice in the baking dish. The water level must reach at least *one inch* before you can cook the veggie rolls.

11. As a finishing touch, add the cheese on top.

12. Cover the baking dish and allow the veggie rolls to cook for at least thirty minutes.

13. Serve the veggie rolls warm to your dog.

Soup of Champions

Ingredients:

- *Whole egg*
- *2 tablespoons of cornstarch (Dissolve the cornstarch in ¼ cup of water first.)*
- *2 tablespoons of tamari sauce*
- *2 tablespoons of parsley*
- *Two scallions (chop these first)*
- *16 ounces of regular tofu*
- *Six to seven cups of regular chicken stock*

Steps:

1. Combine all the ingredients in a pot or medium saucepan.

2. Turn the heat up to medium-heat and allow the mix to simmer for a few minutes.

3. After a quarter of an hour, add the egg and allow the egg to cook thoroughly.

4. Serve warm.

Suave Coat Booster

This recipe produces a puree that can be added to any other dog food you're giving your dog. This puree will help heal any skin problems and will also help keep your dog's coat shiny and healthy.

Ingredients:

- *2 tablespoons of corn oil*
- *Half clove of garlic (crush the garlic before using)*
- *1 tablespoon of brewer's yeast*
- *1/3 cup of wheat germ*
- *1 egg (boil the egg for 4 minutes, keep the shell)*
- *Whole cup of chicken stock*

Steps:

1. Combine all the ingredients in a blender.

2. Blend the ingredients for a minute and store.

3. Pour a small amount of the puree on top of your dog's regular meals.

Festive Dog Food

Ingredients:

- *4-5 slices of bread (cut into small, 1-inch pieces)*
- *2 tablespoons of tamari sauce*
- *Six whole cups of chicken or beef stock*
- *¼ teaspoon of salt*
- *1 tablespoon of oregano*
- *1 whole stalk of fresh celery*
- *2 whole carrots (chop these first before using)*
- *2 onions (chop these first before using)*
- *4 potatoes (sliced into slim, 1-inch thick pieces)*
- *2 tablespoons of butter (non-salted or low salt)*
- *Half kilo of gizzard*

Steps:

1. Fill a pot with water and bring the water to a boil. Pour the gizzards in the water and let the organ meats cook for at least 45 minutes.

2. When the gizzards are cooked, strain the meat but don't throw away the resulting stock. Slice the cooked gizzards.

3. Combine the chicken stock and the soup from the gizzard. Add the sliced gizzards and let the soup cook for an additional ten minutes.

4. Get a medium sized saucepan and put some butter on the pan. Switch the stove to medium heat and cook the butter. Add the vegetables and let the vegetables cook for a few minutes.

5. When the vegetables are cooked, add the vegetables to the soup. The resulting nutritious soup is now ready to be served warm to your dog.

Egg Noodle Deluxe

Ingredients:

- *2 eggs (boil the eggs for four to five minutes then remove the shells before chopping)*
- *Whole cup of bread crumbs*
- *2 tablespoons of parsley*
- *Half cup of cheddar cheese (grate the cheese first)*
- *Whole cup of chicken stock*
- *Two cups of milk*

Bowe Packer

- *Half kilo of egg noodles*
- *Half kilo of chicken or turkey (lean cuts only)*
- *4 tablespoons of butter (low salt or non-salted only)*

Steps:

1. Preheat your oven to 350 degrees Fahrenheit.

2. Add butter to a medium saucepan and cook the shredded turkey or chicken for a few minutes.

3. Cook the egg noodles by following the manufacturer's instruction on the back of the pack.

4. In another pan, combine the milk and the chicken stock. When the mixture is simmering, add the cheddar cheese. Cook the mix until the grated cheddar cheese has melted completely.

5. In a third pan, cook the bread crumbs by toasting the crumbs with butter. Cook for a few minutes and set aside.

6. Mix the resulting cheese soup with the cooked chicken or turkey.

7. Pour the chicken-cheese mix into a baking dish. Add the sliced eggs and the buttery, toasted bread crumbs.

8. Bake the dish for at least 45 minutes. Serve warm.

Lemony Halibut

Ingredients:

- *Cooked rice*
- *2 tablespoons of cilantro*
- *Whole cup of tomato puree (commercial or homemade)*
- *Lemon juice (equivalent to a whole lemon's worth)*
- *Quarter cup of olive oil*
- *1 kilo of halibut steak (deboned)*

Steps:

1. Broil the halibut steaks and season with fresh lemon juice. Use the olive oil, too. Apply with a regular barbecue basting brush.

2. Cook each side for approximately twelve minutes, or until the flesh of the halibut flakes easily with a fork.

Bowe Packer

3. Pour the tomato puree into a medium-sized saucepan and simmer for a few minutes.

4. Place the cooked halibut steaks in your dog's bowl and pour the puree over the halibut. Add cooked rice as well.

Seafood Appetizer

Ingredients:

- *Cooked rice*
- *1 tablespoon of tamari sauce*
- *2 tablespoons of margarine*
- *2 scallions (chop these first)*
- *Whole quart of fish stock*
- *1 kilo of squid*

Steps:

1. Wash and the clean the squid.

2. Add a quart of fish stock to a pot and bring the fish stock to a boil. Add the cleaned squid and cook for 30 minutes.

3. When the squid is cooked, add the rest of the ingredients.

4. Serve warm with cooked rice.

Liver for Life

Ingredients:

- *Dry dog kibble*
- *Bay leaf*
- *Pepper*
- *Whole cup of chicken stock*
- *1 onion (chopped)*
- *3 tablespoons of bacon dripping*
- *1 kilo of beef liver (slice the liver into small pieces first)*
- *Half cup of flour*

Bowe Packer

Steps:

1. Add a little pepper to the flour to add flavor.

2. Coat the sliced beef liver pieces with the peppery flour.

3. Place bacon drippings in a Dutch oven and allow the fat to melt.

4. Add the coated beef liver slices to the melted bacon drippings.

5. Add the rest of the ingredients and let everything cook for at least one hour.

6. Pour the liver and the resulting sauce over your dog's regular food.

Beef & Veggie Pie

Ingredients:

- *Whole cup of chicken stock*
- *2 tablespoons of cornstarch*
- *1 commercial pie crust (nine inches)*
- *1 egg (hard-boiled; remove the shell and slice)*
- *Half cup of beef (ground, low fat)*
- *Two cups of cooked brown rice*
- *1 teaspoon of parsley*
- *1 teaspoon of thyme*
- *1 teaspoon of oregano*
- *Whole cup of broccoli*
- *1 tablespoon of canola oil*

Steps:

1. Preheat your oven to 400 degrees Fahrenheit.

2. Cook the vegetables for a few minutes in a pan or skillet. Add the oil before adding the vegetables.

3. Combine the vegetables with the spices (thyme, oregano, parsley).

4. Dissolve the cornstarch before adding to the chicken stock.

5. Transfer the cooked vegetables to the pie crust. Pour the chicken stock, too.

6. Bake the pie for at least 30 minutes. Serve warm.

ABOUT THE AUTHOR

Hello everyone! My name is Bowe Chaim Packer and I am a bit of a wacky, zany, fun loving guy who does his best to constantly wear his heart out on his sleeve. I must say though, like many of you might already know, it often is challenging in this world that we live in.

Throughout the years I have come to realize the only thing that I can truly be in control of is me. Or shall I say my actions and how I show up in the world. For me it is all about taking responsibility for how I act, how I treat myself and how I treat others. Wheewwwww, and I won't lie, sometimes it takes everything I have to make a decision to act appropriately.

When I do, things always seem to turn out as they should. Funny how that works.!.! ;-)

So, here I am publishing information to the world for consumption. I hope whatever words your read of mine and in whatever format you choose to read them in, that they make a difference in your life. No matter how small or large that difference maybe, it will tell me (in a cosmic kind of way) that I have done my job......

Be sure to always keep your heart open and listening with great intent, for then and only then, you will find what you are looking for in that moment.

Remember, LIFE is a journey for each and every one of us. We must never forget the things that are important to us or lose sight of what makes us happy.

MY COMPLETE PORTFOLIO

Click on the link to check out my complete portfolio: http://amzn.to/1tOkOM9

Includes all formats – paperback, digital (Kindle) and audio for your convenience and preference.

QUESTIONS FOR ME?

Email me @: bowe@sunshineinmysoul.net

AND JUST ONE LAST THING BEFORE WE PART OUR WAYS.....

In life I am coming to understand if you don't ask for what you want, then there is truly no chance of you ever getting it.

With that said, if you are on a Kindle reader, when you turn the page, Kindle will give you an opportunity to rate the book and share your thoughts.

If you believe that your friends and other followers would get something valuable from this book, I would be **honored** if you posted your thoughts.

Also, if you feel particularly strong about the contributions this book made to your life in any way, I would be **eternally grateful** if you posted a review on Amazon. Just go back to your orders within Amazon and click on *"Write a Product Review"* next to the book.

And if you are not on a Kindle reader and would still like to post an Amazon review, well then I would be **delighted, grateful and extremely happy**......

Bowe Packer

All the best to you,

Bowe Chaim Packer

Made in the USA
Middletown, DE
18 August 2022